I LIKE BEING ME

I LIKE BEING ME

Copyright © Summersdale Publishers Ltd, 2023

All rights reserved.

No part of this book may be reproduced by any means, nor transmitted, nor translated into a machine language, without the written permission of the publishers.

Poppy O'Neill has asserted her right to be identified as the author of this work in accordance with sections 77 and 78 of the Copyright, Designs and Patents Act 1988.

Condition of Sale
This book is sold subject to the condition that it shall not, by way of trade or otherwise, be lent, resold, hired out or otherwise circulated in any form of binding or cover other than that in which it is published and without a similar condition including this condition being imposed on the subsequent purchaser.

An Hachette UK Company
www.hachette.co.uk

Vie Books, an imprint of Summersdale Publishers Ltd
Part of Octopus Publishing Group Limited
Carmelite House
50 Victoria Embankment
LONDON
EC4Y 0DZ
UK

www.summersdale.com

Printed and bound in China

ISBN: 978-1-80007-689-1

Substantial discounts on bulk quantities of Summersdale books are available to corporations, professional associations and other organizations. For details contact general enquiries: telephone: +44 (0) 1243 771107 or email: enquiries@summersdale.com.

Neither the author nor the publisher can be held responsible for any loss, damage or injury – be it health, financial or otherwise – arising out of the use, or misuse, of the suggestions made herein.

I LIKE BEING ME

A Child's Guide to Self-Worth

Poppy O'Neill

vie

CONTENTS

Foreword...7
Introduction: A guide for parents and carers......................................8
   Signs your child struggles with low self-worth..............................9
   How to use this book: For parents and carers..............................10
   How to use this book: A guide for children..................................11
Introducing Coco the monster...12

PART 1: JUST AS I AM..13
   Activity: All about me..14
   Activity: Draw your home...16
   Activity: Draw your loved ones...18
   Activity: If I were an animal…..19
   Activity: I'm curious about…..20
   What is self-acceptance?...21
   What is perfectionism?..23
   Activity: Take the perfectionist quiz!..24
   Help Coco..26

PART 2: GETTING TO KNOW PERFECTIONIST THOUGHTS..............29
   Why do we sometimes believe we need to be perfect?.................30
   The inner meanie...32
   Thinking errors..34
   Is it fair or is it perfectionist?..38
   All emotions are OK..40
   Surfing our feelings...41
   Coco needs your help!...44
   Activity: A time I felt the need to be perfect................................46
   Activity: A time I felt good about myself.....................................47

Kind words..48
How perfectionist thoughts make us behave....................49
How to spot perfectionist thoughts.....................................52
Getting curious...53
Curiosity cards...55

PART 3: IT'S OK TO BE ME...58

Mindfulness..59
Activity: Try a breathing track...61
Being kind to yourself..64
Activity: One-minute visualization......................................67
Who can I talk to?...68
Talk about your feelings...69
Activity: Write about your feelings....................................70
Get moving!..73
Activity: Draw your happy place!.......................................75
Getting comfy with not knowing..77
Self-acceptance at school..78

PART 4: GOODBYE PERFECT!...81

What I can and can't control...82
How to press pause..83
Thinking differently about mistakes..................................85
Useful mistakes..87
Being yourself..90
Activity: Get creative..92
Activity: Finding gratitude..94
Activity: What is self-talk?..96
Activity: Tell a new story..98
Activity: Get scribbling...100
Self-acceptance tool kit..102

PART 5: TAKING CARE OF YOU 104

How are you doing? 105
Activity: Yoga stretches 106
Making time to chill 108
Activity: Paint a messy monster 111
Yummy, healthy food 114
Activity: Build your own bruschetta 115
Screen-free time 117
Getting a good night's sleep 119
Asking for help 120

PART 6: CELEBRATE YOURSELF 122

I'm proud of… 123
Activity: Spread self-acceptance 125
Playing your part 127
Helping your friends 129
Make a promise to yourself 131
I Like Being Me golden rules 132
Stories of self-acceptance 133
The end 135

For parents and carers: How to help build your child's self-acceptance 137
Further advice 139
Recommended reading 140

FOREWORD

Amanda Ashman-Wymbs
Counsellor and Psychotherapist, registered and accredited by
the British Association for Counselling and Psychotherapy

I have worked with children for many years in the public and private sector, and it is clear to me that many children today find it hard to live up to perfectionist ideas they have picked up about who they should be, how they should look or what they should be achieving. As a result, they struggle with issues of self-acceptance and self-esteem when faced with the reality of being their unique and natural self.

I Like Being Me by Poppy O'Neill is a great little workbook, which will really support a child to be kinder to themselves and more respectful of their uniqueness. Through easy-to-understand text and fun activities they will learn how they may be trying to live up to perfectionist narratives in their heads, how to be more self-accepting, think more positively and realistically, and honour their individuality.

This book encourages a child's curiosity about, and understanding of, their inner world. It prompts them to speak about what they are experiencing with a trusted adult and offers many other useful tools to help them to cope, both at home and at school. The exercises cover topics such as an introduction to mindfulness techniques, reflection on gratitude, being creative, relaxing, connecting with the environment and cutting down screen time. There are exercises that help the child to understand the importance of maintaining a healthy lifestyle, and others that show them how to be aware of, and deal with, difficult emotions and thought processes. It sensitively supports the reader, building their confidence to make positive changes and feel good about themselves just as they are.

INTRODUCTION: A GUIDE FOR PARENTS AND CARERS

All children – and a lot of grown-ups! – struggle with self-worth sometimes. It can be really tough to cut ourselves some slack when we're struggling or make a mistake. Comparing ourselves with others is another reason we can find it difficult to accept ourselves as we are. This book uses simple, engaging activities and methods drawn from child psychology – including cognitive behavioural therapy and mindfulness techniques – to help your child grow their self-acceptance.

You may have noticed that your child seems to feel more anxious than others, or perhaps they appear to be more concerned than usual with fitting in or keeping up with their friends. Sometimes it doesn't matter how much you remind them they are wonderful, they never feel quite good enough!

This book is aimed at children aged 7–11 – a time of great change and development in terms of their minds, bodies, academic and social lives; all of which can have an impact on their still-forming sense of self. They'll experience exams for the first time, close friendships will form and as their awareness of their bodies develops they may begin to compare their attractiveness with others'. It's also a time when some children get their first experiences of puberty, peer pressure and social media. Messages about what traits and body types are desirable and undesirable start to filter in from the outside world. It's very understandable that some children might need help maintaining a healthy sense of self-acceptance during all these changes.

So, if you feel that your child may be struggling with perfectionism and could benefit from some help accepting and loving themselves as they are, rest assured that you're not alone and you have the power to help them.

INTRODUCTION: A GUIDE FOR PARENTS AND CARERS

Signs your child struggles with low self-worth and perfectionism

To help determine if your child has trouble with perfectionism, look out for these habits:

- They are reluctant to try new or challenging things

- They compare themselves with others (favourably or unfavourably)

- They are self-critical and hard on themselves

- They seem unsure of themselves and unable to make choices

- They have a strong emotional reaction when they make a mistake

- They seem to look outside themselves for direction

Try keeping a diary of when you notice these signs. It could be that there's a specific situation, place or person that makes self-acceptance difficult for your child. This way you can be better equipped to help your child.

The important thing to remember is that it's never too late to start helping your child feel comfortable and accepting of themselves.

How to use this book: For parents and carers

Introduce your child to this book and let them set the pace. They might like to read it with you or alone. Either way, see if you can get them talking about the things they learn and their thoughts and feelings about it.

The activities are designed to get children thinking about how they relate to themselves and the world around them, as well as encouraging creativity and celebrating differences. When your child feels secure in themselves they are better equipped to deal with the challenges of everyday life. Let them know that you love and support them exactly as they are, and that you trust them to know their own mind.

I hope this book helps your child to feel free and comfortable to be themselves, enabling greater understanding of their own mind and the things that might knock their sense of self-acceptance. However, if you have serious worries about your child's self-image and mental health, your GP is the best person to go to for further advice.

HOW TO USE THIS BOOK: A GUIDE FOR CHILDREN

This book is for you if you often…

- Feel like you need to be perfect
- Find it hard to say what you really think and feel
- Feel like you aren't as good as other people
- Worry that you're very different from everyone else

If that sounds like you sometimes, or all of the time, you're not the only one. This book is for anyone who has a hard time being themselves. It's packed with activities and ideas that will help you feel more comfortable with yourself and raise your self-worth.

You can read through the book at your own pace… there's no rush! There might be parts of the book that you'd like to talk through with a grown-up you trust and feel good talking to, and that's fine. This book is about you, so there are no wrong answers. You are the expert on you and this book is here to help you see just how wonderful it is to be you, exactly as you are!

INTRODUCING COCO THE MONSTER

Hi there! I'm Coco and I'm excited to meet you! There are loads of fun activities and interesting ideas in this book, and I'll be here to learn along with you. Are you ready? Let's get started.

PART 1: JUST AS I AM

There's only one you and you're brilliant! In this chapter we're going to learn all about you and all about self-acceptance. Getting to know yourself is a really important part of accepting who you are and building your confidence.

I like being me!

I LIKE BEING ME

ACTIVITY: ALL ABOUT ME

Can you complete the sentences so Coco can get to know you better?

My name is...

I am __ years old.

I feel happy when...

I feel excited when...

I feel angry when...

PART 1: JUST AS I AM

I feel worried about...

I feel good about...

I feel sad about...

My least favourite thing to do is...

My favourite thing to do is...

I LIKE BEING ME

ACTIVITY: DRAW YOUR HOME

Our homes are where we can relax and be ourselves. Can you draw your house on the facing page? You could draw the outside, inside, a map… you decide!

Answer these questions to get you thinking about your favourite things about home.

- Which is your favourite room?
- Do you have a chair you like best?
- Where is the sunniest place in your home?

PART 1: JUST AS I AM

I LIKE BEING ME

ACTIVITY: DRAW YOUR LOVED ONES

Who are the people that you love to spend time with? It might be people in your family, friends from school or someone else.

Can you transform the outlines below into some of your favourite people?

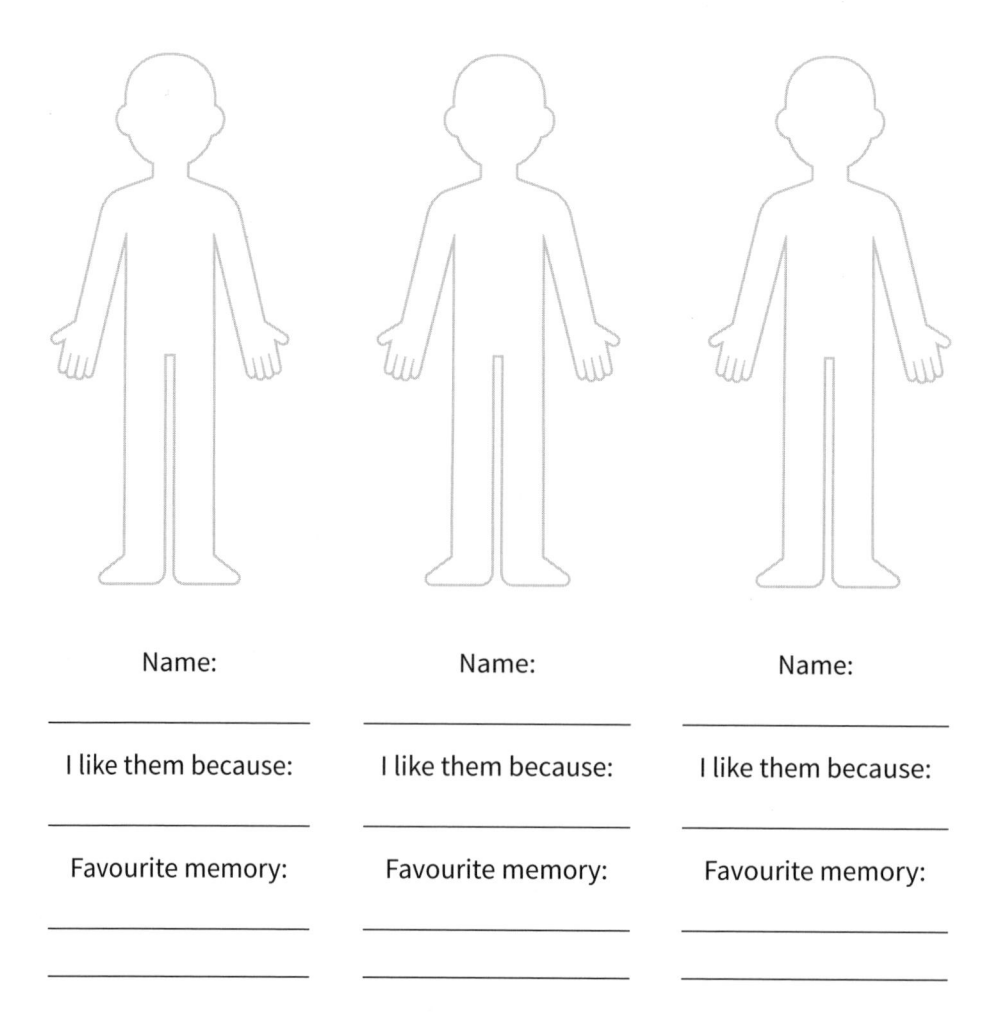

Name:

_____

I like them because:

_____

Favourite memory:

_____

_____

Name:

_____

I like them because:

_____

Favourite memory:

_____

_____

Name:

_____

I like them because:

_____

Favourite memory:

_____

_____

PART 1: JUST AS I AM

ACTIVITY: IF I WERE AN ANIMAL...

If you were an animal, what would you be? Write or draw about yourself as an animal here!

I would be a...

I would be one because...

I'd look like this:

I LIKE BEING ME

ACTIVITY: I'M CURIOUS ABOUT...

Coco is very curious about plants. Coco likes to read about plants and look at them carefully as Coco is growing a tomato plant from a seed at home.

What are you curious about? It might be a book, a science topic, someone from history, an artist or something you collect. Everybody is different and we're all interested in different things!

Write or draw about your interest or interests here:

PART 1: JUST AS I AM

WHAT IS SELF-ACCEPTANCE?

Self-acceptance means feeling OK about yourself. It can be difficult to feel good about yourself sometimes. Many kids your age struggle when they:

- Make a mistake

- Compare themselves with others

- Are around someone who is angry

- Are learning something new

- Don't look the way they want

- Don't come first or get the top grade

- Feel big emotions

- Go somewhere new

This is because when we feel like we don't fit in or feel like we aren't good enough, our thoughts sometimes tell us that we need to change ourselves or try harder in order for others to accept and welcome us.

When we build self-acceptance, we learn to remember that even when we are not perfect, we are OK, and still deserve kindness and understanding.

I AM ALWAYS GROWING AND LEARNING

PART 1: JUST AS I AM

WHAT IS PERFECTIONISM?

Perfectionism is a long word that means believing you need to be perfect in order to have friendships, kindness and understanding. It's very hard to be yourself if you have this belief, because no one is perfect... perfect doesn't actually exist.

Perfectionism makes you think you need to be...

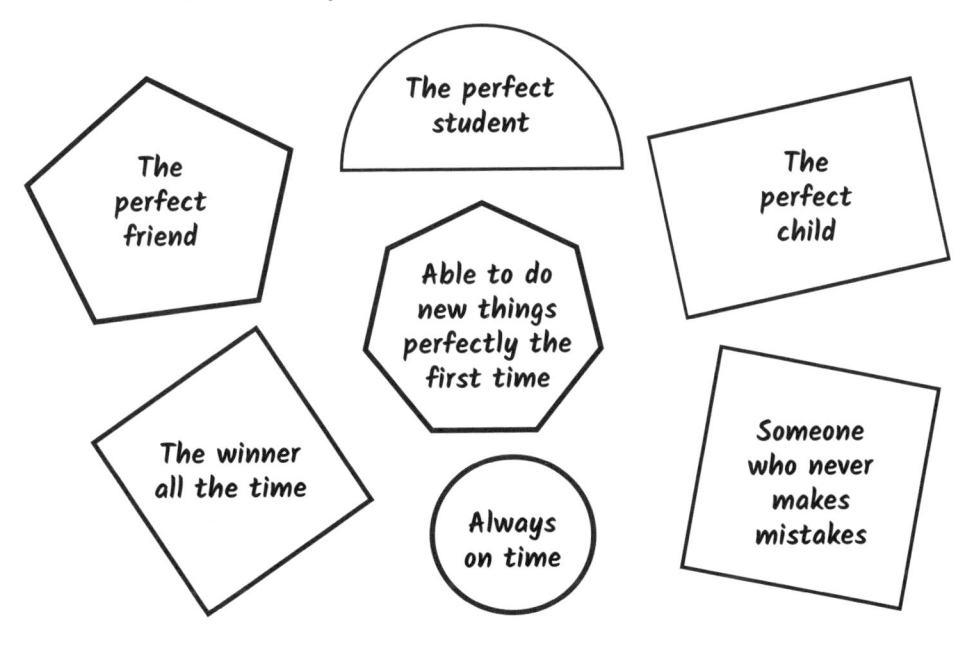

- The perfect student
- The perfect friend
- The perfect child
- Able to do new things perfectly the first time
- The winner all the time
- Always on time
- Someone who never makes mistakes

Even if we know in our minds that nothing bad will really happen, perfectionism can cause big feelings of anxiety in our bodies. If you believe you need to be perfect, the idea of getting something wrong can be really scary.

The good news is that learning about perfectionism helps us beat it. When we can spot ourselves believing that we need to be perfect, we can choose a different belief. Keep reading to find out how!

23

ACTIVITY: TAKE THE PERFECTIONIST QUIZ!

This quiz will help you find out if perfectionist beliefs are giving you a hard time. Circle one answer for each question, then read your results at the end.

1. When I'm working on something, I…
a. Keep going until it's perfect
b. Get angry if I make a mistake
c. Do my best and make improvements as I go

2. I worry most about…
a. Messing up and getting things wrong
b. What other people think of me
c. Things that happen in my life, like falling out with friends

3. I find it hard when…
a. I'm not the best at something
b. Everyone's attention is on me
c. I'm not feeling interested or challenged by what I'm doing

4. When I make a mistake…
a. I feel angry with myself
b. I feel embarrassed
c. It's not a nice feeling, but it's easy for me to try again

PART 1: JUST AS I AM

5. When I need help, I…
a. Find it very hard to ask for it
b. Try to copy my friend
c. Find it easy to ask for it

6. I play games in order to…
a. Win
b. Try my best
c. Have fun

Mostly A: You're very hard on yourself and you believe you should be perfect all the time! Keep reading to find out more about perfectionist thoughts, how to be kinder to yourself and why you learn more when you make mistakes.

Mostly B: You worry a lot about what other people think about you. You're a caring person and you often feel like you're letting your friends down if you're not perfect or need help. It's OK to be you, exactly as you are. Read on to learn why perfection doesn't exist and how true friends will be there for you, even if you mess up.

Mostly C: You're pretty kind to yourself and being perfect isn't a huge deal for you. We all have trouble with self-acceptance sometimes and there are times you find it hard to see the positives. This book will help you learn all about your emotions and how to accept yourself, no matter what.

I LIKE BEING ME

HELP COCO

Coco has drawn a picture of a horse. Coco used a photo in a book to copy from. But Coco's picture doesn't look exactly like the photo.

Coco feels really down!

I can't do it – I should just give up!

What would be the best thing for Coco to do?

💜　Never draw again

💜　Keep trying

💜　Be kinder to themselves

PART 1: JUST AS I AM

Coco could give up drawing forever, but Coco enjoys drawing and would lose a favourite hobby. What's more, Coco will never learn how to draw a more realistic horse without practice!

Coco could keep trying – that's a good idea. But if Coco's feeling big emotions, it's best to take a short break before trying again.

Coco could be kinder to themselves – yes! Speaking kindly to yourself is so important. Coco doesn't need to be perfect, Coco just needs to be Coco.

What kind words could Coco use?

IT'S GREAT BEING ME

PART 2: GETTING TO KNOW PERFECTIONIST THOUGHTS

Learning how to spot unkind and unfair thoughts is the first step to overcoming them. In this chapter we'll find out why we sometimes believe we need to be perfect and what perfectionist thoughts can sound like.

WHY DO WE SOMETIMES BELIEVE WE NEED TO BE PERFECT?

Our brains are always working to keep us safe from difficult emotions and pain. Often, when we think of a time when we felt sad, angry or scared, or our bodies got hurt, it happened after something we did wasn't perfect.

For example:

"I was looking at an interesting cloud when I tripped on a tree root and dropped my ice cream. I hurt my knee and felt sad that my ice cream was gone."

Bad luck and accidents happen, because the world is not perfect. But our brains like to imagine that we can protect ourselves by acting differently next time. Sometimes this is true – like if we wait too long to eat an ice cream, it will melt – so our brains remind us to eat it more quickly next time!

If your brain is thinking perfectionist thoughts, it might say:

I need to look at the ground all the time, in case I trip!

I must look at my ice cream all the time, in case something bad happens to it!

PART 2: GETTING TO KNOW PERFECTIONIST THOUGHTS

> I shouldn't have an ice cream, because the last one I had fell on the ground.

> I shouldn't have an ice cream, because I'll be too upset if I lose it.

Can you see how the perfectionist thoughts are the brain's way of trying to keep you safe from getting hurt and feeling sad again?

These thoughts might work – if you never have another ice cream, your ice cream will never fall on the ground again. But that means no more ice cream! Having a fun, happy and interesting life means hard things will happen sometimes, and you'll feel difficult emotions. The trick is to learn to cope with hard things, not to give up on the fun, happy and interesting things.

THE INNER MEANIE

Perfectionist thoughts often come from something called an "inner critic" – Coco likes to call it the inner meanie. The inner meanie is like a character that pops up in your thoughts when you're being brave and tries to make you feel bad about yourself – what a meanie!

The inner meanie says things like…

You need to be perfect.

You shouldn't even try.

You're not good enough.

Everyone is laughing at you.

The inner meanie gets bigger and stronger when we believe what it tells us and when we hear unkind words from others. The inner meanie makes perfectionist thoughts sound very real and important – it's sneaky like that.

PART 2: GETTING TO KNOW PERFECTIONIST THOUGHTS

How to shrink your inner meanie

You don't need to listen to your inner meanie – shrinking its voice helps.

Give it a name
Naming your inner meanie something silly makes it less scary and easier to ignore. Write your inner meanie's name here:

The best friend test
When you spot a mean thought, ask: would I say this to my best friend? If you wouldn't, it's not fair to think it about yourself!

Tell on your meanie
When your inner meanie gets loud and difficult to ignore, tell a trusted grown-up that you're having trouble with it. Talking about your inner meanie makes it a lot less powerful.

I LIKE BEING ME

THINKING ERRORS

When we're feeling big emotions, our brain can come up with negative stories about what's happening. These are called "thinking errors" and they're our inner meanie talking.

These are some of the most common thinking errors and what they can sound like:

ALL-OR-NOTHING THINKING: if something isn't perfect, I've failed completely.

FOCUSING ON THE NEGATIVE: I can only see the bad parts — even when something nice happens, I always find a way to feel bad about it.

FORTUNE-TELLING: I know something will go wrong, so I won't try.

MIND-READING: I know everyone will think badly of me.

MAGNIFIED THINKING: If a small, bad thing happens, it feels really big and important.

PART 2: GETTING TO KNOW PERFECTIONIST THOUGHTS

> **COMPARING YOURSELF WITH OTHERS:** my friend is better than me in every way.

> **UNREALISTIC EXPECTATIONS:** I should be perfect at everything.

> **PUTTING YOURSELF DOWN:** I'm rubbish!

> **BLAMING YOURSELF:** everything goes wrong and it's all my fault.

> **FEELINGS ARE FACTS:** I feel bad, so I must BE bad at everything I do.

Do any of these sound like your inner meanie? Colour in any that you recognize.

Perfect doesn't exist

Did you notice that a lot of the thinking errors are about being perfect? Thinking errors make us believe that we need to be perfect in order to have friendships, be treated fairly and with kindness.

The truth is, nobody is perfect and no matter how hard you work or how much you try, you won't ever be perfect either. Not because there is something wrong with you, but because perfect doesn't exist.

For Coco, the perfect ice cream sundae has three scoops of banana, one scoop of vanilla, chocolate sauce and a strawberry on top.

For Coco's friend Glow, the perfect ice cream sundae has two scoops of chocolate, two scoops of strawberry, whipped cream and a chocolate flake.

Neither ice cream sundae is actually perfect, because everyone has different opinions! It's the same with people. As long as you like yourself, that's all you need.

What's your perfect ice cream sundae? Colour in the sundaes for you, Coco and Glow!

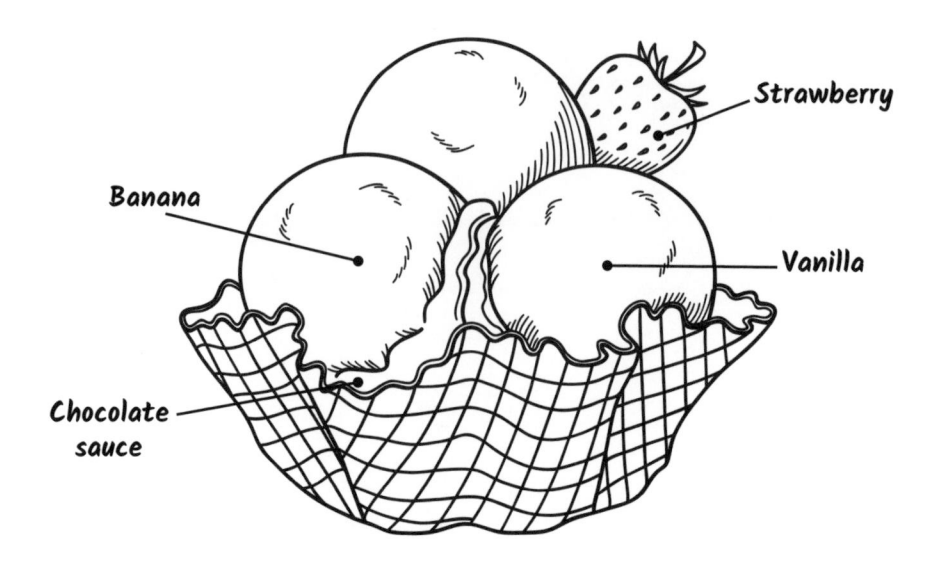

PART 2: GETTING TO KNOW PERFECTIONIST THOUGHTS

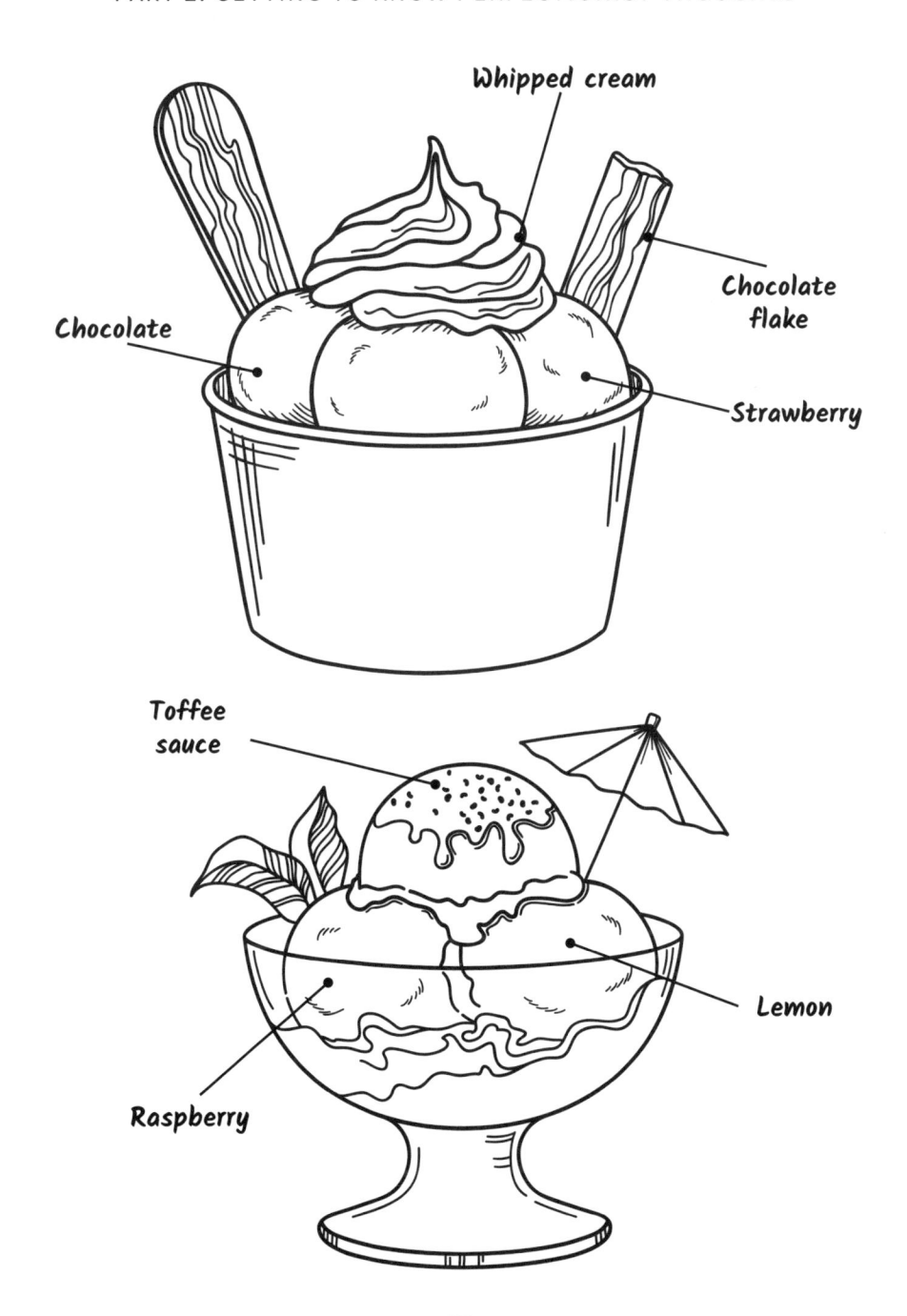

- Whipped cream
- Chocolate
- Chocolate flake
- Strawberry
- Toffee sauce
- Lemon
- Raspberry

IS IT FAIR OR IS IT PERFECTIONIST?

We're always learning and getting more skilled, but there's a big difference between thoughts that are perfectionist and thoughts that are about growing our skills and improving.

Here's how to tell the difference between a fair thought and an unfair one:

A fair thought...	An unfair thought...
...sees how hard you're trying	...sees only your mistakes
...is kind	...is unkind
...helps you work things out at your own pace	...tells you what you should do
...is patient	...wants you to be perfect right this instant
...has ideas about the next step	...makes you want to give up
...is about the thing you're working on	...tells you there's something wrong with you
...is helpful	...makes you feel stuck

PART 2: GETTING TO KNOW PERFECTIONIST THOUGHTS

Are these thoughts fair or unfair? Draw a circle around your answers:

FAIR	I'm bad at this! I should give up.	UNFAIR
FAIR	I wonder how I could make my picture more colourful?	UNFAIR
FAIR	I'm getting in everybody's way, I should just go.	UNFAIR
FAIR	I got that one wrong, let's work out what happened.	UNFAIR
FAIR	I could have been a better friend today – how could I make it right?	UNFAIR
FAIR	I should just be quiet, everybody else knows how to do this.	UNFAIR

Did you spot the unfair thoughts? There's one word that often pops up in unfair, perfectionist thoughts and it's in all three of the examples. The word is "should".

When the word "should" is part of our thoughts, it often means they're unfair thoughts.

> **If you spot a perfectionist thought, don't panic! Here's a trick for perfectionist thoughts:**
> Write it on a piece of scrap paper and throw it in the bin!
> Doing this helps move the thought out of your brain.

ALL EMOTIONS ARE OK

Everyone feels emotions all day long – even if they don't show them on the outside. Most people don't show every emotion they have, so when you're feeling a difficult emotion it can seem like you're the only one.

Sometimes, feelings of low self-worth can make you believe that you shouldn't show your emotions on the outside, because your feelings might upset somebody else. This is your inner meanie talking – remember that it *is* OK to show your feelings and to share them with others.

Even when you're feeling something tricky – like anger, sadness or worry – it's OK for you to feel this way.

How are you feeling right now? Write or draw about your feelings here:

PART 2: GETTING TO KNOW PERFECTIONIST THOUGHTS

SURFING OUR FEELINGS

Feelings aren't right or wrong, they're just messages from our bodies. Building self-acceptance is all about being OK with all feelings – even the difficult ones like anger and worry.

When we accept our feelings and let ourselves feel them, they usually pass quite quickly – about a minute and a half according to brain scientists. Learning how to feel emotions until they pass helps us to make calm choices and not act in ways we later regret.

It can help to think of feelings like waves or mountains – the feeling gets bigger and bigger, then starts to feel easier and calmer, until they fade away. Some emotions feel quite uncomfortable so it's not easy!

Taking deep breaths will help you ride out the emotion like a surfer on a wave.

I LIKE BEING ME

Jem has won a prize in the art competition! Coco's painting didn't win a prize and Coco feels angry about it.

Coco's anger feels really uncomfortable. Coco says something hurtful to Jem!

You must have cheated

Let's try that again – this time, Coco imagines surfing the angry feeling like a surfer on a wave.

The anger feels uncomfortable for Coco. Coco takes a deep breath and thinks some kind words.

It's OK to feel angry and disappointed

Coco's angry feeling starts to get smaller, easier and calmer.

Another deep breath and it has faded away.

Coco feels calm now.

Well done, Jem!

MY FEELINGS MATTER

I LIKE BEING ME

COCO NEEDS YOUR HELP!

During the summer break, Coco read four books and Blip read ten books.

Coco feels not good enough, because Blip read more books! Coco's inner meanie is saying:

- Blip is better than you
- Why didn't you read as many books as Blip?
- You should have read more quickly

PART 2: GETTING TO KNOW PERFECTIONIST THOUGHTS

Even though it isn't a competition and Coco had fun reading four interesting books, those perfectionist thoughts are coming up in Coco's mind.
What kind words could help Coco?

- I am not in competition, we are all unique and wonderful
- It's OK to be different
- Nobody is perfect
- It's OK to feel upset

What would you say to help Coco feel OK?

//I LIKE BEING ME

ACTIVITY: A TIME I FELT THE NEED TO BE PERFECT

Can you think of a time your inner meanie made you believe you needed to be perfect?

Write or draw about it here:

PART 2: GETTING TO KNOW PERFECTIONIST THOUGHTS

ACTIVITY: A TIME I FELT GOOD ABOUT MYSELF

Can you think of a time you felt good, proud and happy to be you? Write or draw about it here:

I LIKE BEING ME

KIND WORDS

We can use kind words to quieten our inner meanie and its perfectionist thoughts. Here are some kinder words we can say out loud or in our heads: Instead of being perfect, I can…

- Be good enough
- Try my best
- Be OK as I am
- Try new things
- Like myself when I fail
- Like myself when I succeed
- Be proud of my effort
- Remember perfect doesn't exist
- Pay attention to the present moment
- Feel lucky to be me

PART 2: GETTING TO KNOW PERFECTIONIST THOUGHTS

HOW PERFECTIONIST THOUGHTS MAKE US BEHAVE

Believing that we need to be perfect can make us act in ways that hold us back from enjoying life. Here are some of them:

Avoidance: Hiding from or choosing not to do something, because we are afraid of getting it wrong.

When we avoid trying things, we don't give ourselves the chance to find out what will really happen. If you try, you have a chance at fun, success and learning. If you don't try, you'll never know and your self-acceptance can't grow.

Can you think of a time you were really brave? Write or draw about it here:

Hiding: Keeping the things that make us different a secret from others, in order to fit in or appear perfect.

A true friend likes you because you are uniquely you! Without the things that make us different, friendships wouldn't really work – you need unique people to make a friendship interesting, fun and trusting. True friends are lucky to know the real you!

Can you think of a time you learned something surprising about a friend? Write or draw about it here:

Being passive: Trying to please others all the time and not feeling able to say "no" to things you don't want to do.

Standing up for yourself can be scary. Sometimes it feels easier to let others get their way and keep your own feelings a secret. Perfectionist thoughts make us believe that we can be perfect by caring about others more than ourselves, but it's not true. Standing up for yourself means being kind to yourself and others.

Can you think of a time you stood up for yourself or a friend? Write or draw about it here:

I AM BRILLIANTLY, IMPERFECTLY, WONDERFULLY ME!

I LIKE BEING ME

HOW TO SPOT PERFECTIONIST THOUGHTS

Perfectionist thoughts can be very sneaky. It's easy to think we're being kind or trying our best when actually we're being quite unkind to ourselves.

Coco gets a maths problem wrong:

> *I'm so stupid!*
> *I have to remember better next time*
> *– no more mistakes allowed.*

Coco thinks this thought will lead to fewer mistakes in future, but does this thought help solve the next maths problem? Probably not. The thought just makes Coco feel worried about making another mistake.

Perfectionist thoughts don't help us to become more perfect or make fewer mistakes, they just make us a little bit more scared and a little bit less resilient.

Perfectionist thoughts are:

Unkind –
they make you feel embarrassed or ashamed of yourself

Unhelpful –
they don't help you learn

Uncurious –
they don't help you think through what happened

Let's try it again.

Coco gets a maths problem wrong:

> *Hmm, what went wrong?*

Now Coco is being curious about the mistake. Coco isn't feeling worried, embarrassed or scared, which means Coco is able to use the mistake to learn more about the maths problem.

PART 2: GETTING TO KNOW PERFECTIONIST THOUGHTS

GETTING CURIOUS

Curiosity is a superpower that can beat perfectionism! When you get curious, you can take a look at your mistakes, differences and actions without being unkind to yourself.

Curiosity asks questions like:

- Is anything wrong or are we just different?
- Why did that just happen?
- Where has this feeling come from?
- How can I find out more?
- Do I need to say sorry?
- Does this feel OK to me?

I LIKE BEING ME

Imagine a child you don't know asked to borrow your ball. Perfectionist thoughts might say, "You need to give them the ball, then they might want to be friends."

Instead, let's ask some curious questions – write your ideas below.

Do I need to find out more? What questions could I ask them?

E.g. How long do you want to borrow it for? What game do you want to play?

Once you've asked some curious questions, you can ask yourself, "How does this feel for me? Do I want to say yes or no?"

PART 2: GETTING TO KNOW PERFECTIONIST THOUGHTS

CURIOSITY CARDS

Curiosity isn't just a superpower for beating perfectionism – it's useful any time. Showing curiosity helps us build great friendships, learn about the world and understand our feelings better.

Carefully cut out these curiosity cards and use them to start a curious conversation!

What is your favourite book?	What's the best thing you saw today?
Tell me a fact I might not know	What do you think clouds smell like?
What's one thing you're learning about?	If you could live anywhere, where would you live?

I LIKE BEING ME

EVERYBODY IS UNIQUE!

PART 3: IT'S OK TO BE ME

Learning to like and accept yourself exactly as you are isn't always easy! Our brains can be filled with unkind thoughts that don't help us to do this. In this chapter you'll find lots of activities that will help grow your self-acceptance.

I accept myself!

PART 3: IT'S OK TO BE ME

MINDFULNESS

Practising mindfulness means focusing your attention on the present moment. Using mindfulness helps us to feel calm and learn to see through unhelpful thoughts, and know that they are just thoughts, so we don't need to pay attention to them. A big part of being mindful is accepting things the way they are and that includes us, too!

The simplest way to try mindfulness for yourself is by breathing mindfully. Here's how:

- 💜 Close your eyes and concentrate on the feeling of breathing in and out.

- 💜 Notice how the air feels moving in and out of your nostrils.

- 💜 See if you can breathe a little deeper and notice how that feels.

- 💜 Keep going for three more breaths.

You just used mindfulness! How did it make you feel?

I LIKE BEING ME

We can use mindfulness for dealing with big emotions and unhelpful thoughts. When you're having trouble feeling calm or being kind to yourself, focus on your breathing or try one of these mindful activities.

Mindful feet
Place your feet flat on the ground and focus your attention on what you can feel through the soles of your feet.

What does the ground or floor feel like? Is it warm or cool, bumpy or smooth?

Five senses challenge
Bring your attention to each of your five senses and count five things you can see, four things you can touch, three things you can hear, two things you can smell and one thing you can taste.

Mindfully seeing
Choose something to look at – it could be a picture on the wall, a toy or even your own hand – and look at it very carefully. Notice its shape, texture, colour, all the small details.

Mindful humming
Make a humming noise – it could be a tune or just a sound – and notice how it feels in your mouth, throat and chest.

PART 3: IT'S OK TO BE ME

ACTIVITY: TRY A BREATHING TRACK

Perfectionist thoughts can make you feel panic and anxiety. Breathing slowly and deeply as you follow the breathing tracks on this page will calm your mind and body, helping the perfectionist thoughts disappear.

Put your finger at the start of each of these breathing tracks and slowly trace your finger around the track as you breathe in and out.

> **You can come back to this page any time you want to do some deep breathing, or make your own with a piece of card! You can even trace a shape with one finger on the palm of your hand if you don't have this book with you.**

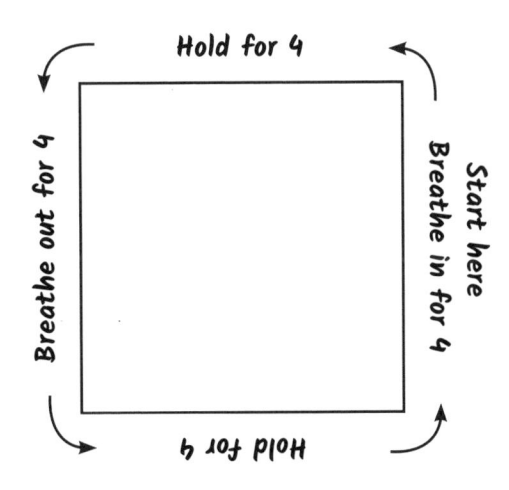

Hold for 4

Breathe out for 4

Start here
Breathe in for 4

Hold for 4

I LIKE BEING ME

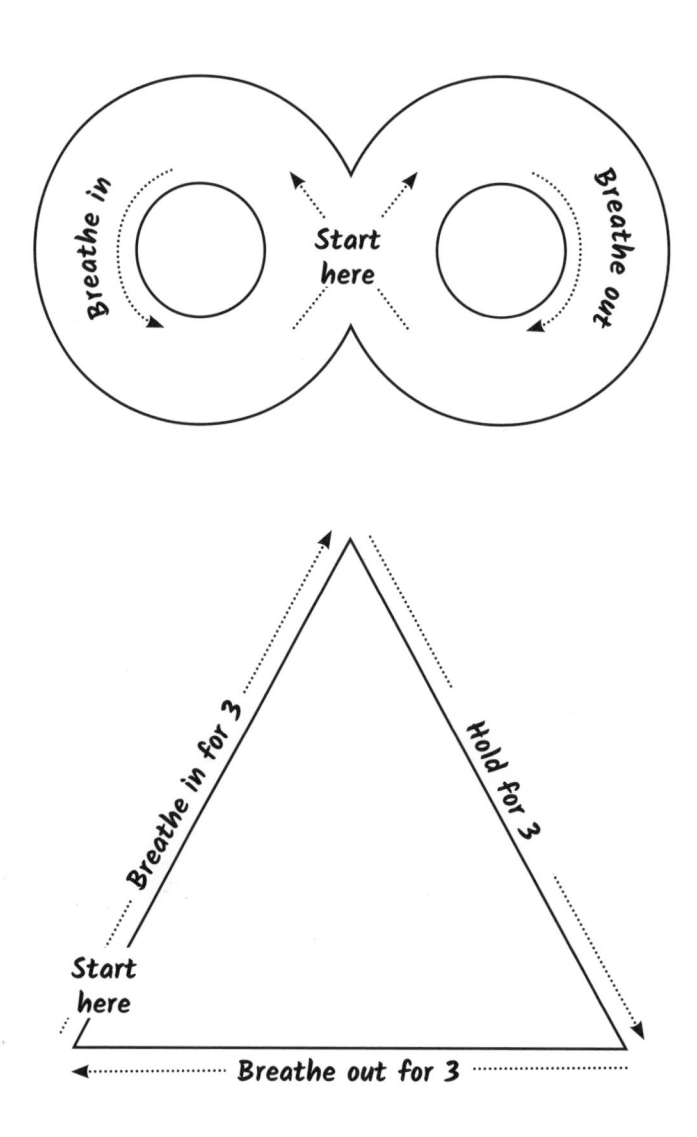

Breathe in
Start here
Breathe out

Breathe in for 3
Hold for 3
Start here
Breathe out for 3

I FEEL CALM AND CONFIDENT IN MY ABILITIES

I LIKE BEING ME

BEING KIND TO YOURSELF

It's not easy having an inner meanie telling you that you need to be perfect all the time. Luckily, we can find other, kinder voices inside of our minds too. Finding a kinder voice inside means showing ourselves kindness and understanding, especially when we're having a hard time.

A kind inner voice might say things like:

- You're being so brave
- You did well today
- You are doing your best
- Your feelings matter
- This is hard!
- I'm proud of you

You gave your inner meanie a name on page 33, now it's time to give your inner kind voice a name.

What will you call your inner kind voice?

PART 3: IT'S OK TO BE ME

Just like anything new, finding an inner kind voice takes practice. It might be tricky at first to remember to use your inner kind voice when you're having a hard time, instead of listening to your inner meanie. Keep going, because it gets easier the more you practice.

Having reminders around your home will help you get used to using your inner kind voice. Colour in the kind words, then carefully cut them out and ask a grown-up to help you put them in places like your bedroom, on the fridge and by your front door.

There's no need to rush	Perfect doesn't exist
My best is enough	I am free to be me
Take things one step at a time	I am brave, kind and curious

I LIKE BEING ME

PART 3: IT'S OK TO BE ME

ACTIVITY: ONE-MINUTE VISUALIZATION

When you want to relax and show yourself kindness, try a one-minute visualization like this one. You can read it then set a timer and picture yourself as a river, or ask someone to read it to you in a calm, gentle voice:

Sit somewhere comfortable and close your eyes. Imagine you are a shimmering fish in a calm, slow-flowing river. The sun is shining on you and you are swimming past a beautiful field, with rabbits sitting either side of the river and eating buttercups. You flow gently without having to try, there's no rush to get anywhere or do anything.

A family of ducks is swimming in the river and you swim around them, feeling their orange feet tickle you. A little further along, there's a small island. Whatever obstacles are in the river, you simply swim with the flow of the water around them with ease. You flow past the island, where a mother swan is keeping her eggs warm in its nest.

You make your way along the river, it's calm and quiet, and sometimes there's a boat with splashing oars or a low tree branch dipping itself into the river. Whatever happens, you feel calm and you continue to swim with the water's flow. Stay imagining yourself as a fish for as long as you like, and when you're ready you can start to wiggle your fingers and toes. Now you can open your eyes, take a deep breath and go back to your day.

WHO CAN I TALK TO?

Think about the person or people in your life that you feel calm and comfortable around, and that you trust. You don't need to trust someone just because they're kind to you – trust is a feeling inside you.

A trusted person might be a school friend, brother or sister or a grown-up. A trusted grown-up could be a parent, carer, teacher, neighbour, family member or someone else – they're grown-ups who are good listeners and who care about you. You might have lots of people you feel OK talking to, or maybe just one or two.

Write or draw about your trusted people here:

PART 3: IT'S OK TO BE ME

TALK ABOUT YOUR FEELINGS

Perfectionist thoughts can make us believe we need to keep our feelings a secret, in case they upset or annoy someone else. But it's not true! The people who love you want to know how you're doing and what it's like to be you.

Talking about your feelings is the number one way of making emotions feel easier and lighter. It can be tricky to know where to start, so try one of these handy conversation starters…

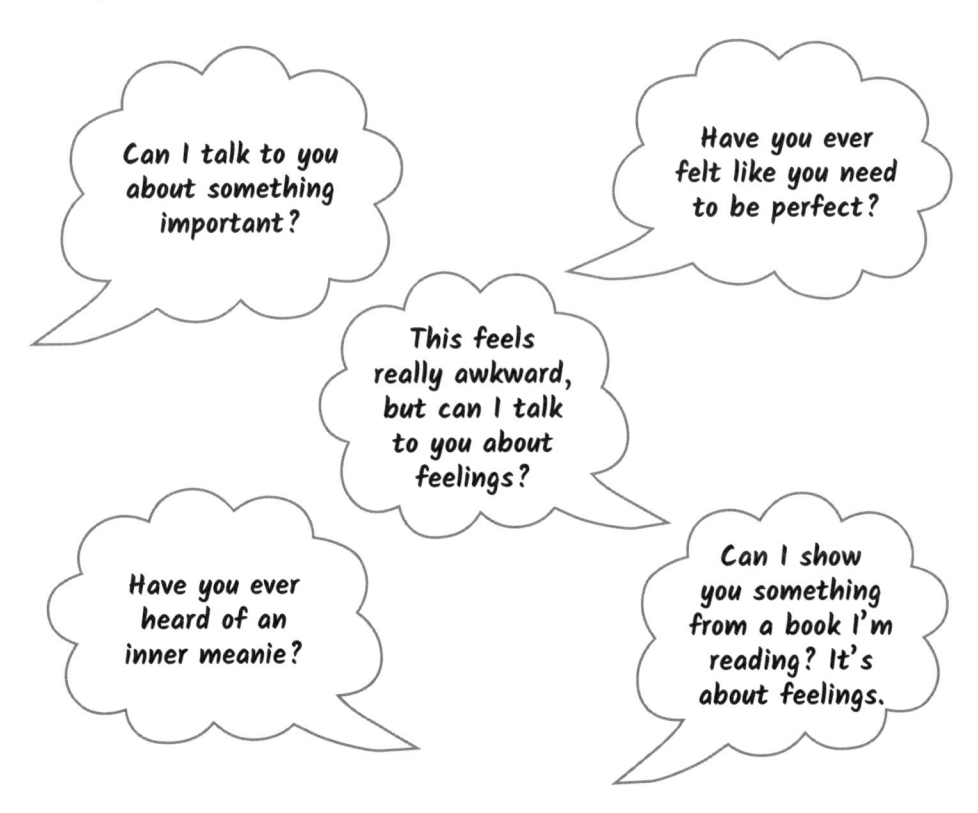

Can I talk to you about something important?

Have you ever felt like you need to be perfect?

This feels really awkward, but can I talk to you about feelings?

Have you ever heard of an inner meanie?

Can I show you something from a book I'm reading? It's about feelings.

ACTIVITY: WRITE ABOUT YOUR FEELINGS

Your feelings are a big part of what makes you special. Everybody has their own feelings and even though they can be tricky, having feelings is what makes life interesting.

Writing about how you are feeling is a good way to help yourself feel calm and make sense of tricky emotions. Try keeping a journal every day for a week and see how it feels! You could write in your journal after school, before going to bed or whenever feels right.

Monday
Today I felt……………………………………………………………………
I was proud of myself when……………………………………………
……………………………………………………………………………………

Tuesday
Today I felt……………………………………………………………………
What I learned today:……………………………………………………
……………………………………………………………………………………

PART 3: IT'S OK TO BE ME

Wednesday

Today I felt..

I'm grateful for...

....

Thursday

Today I felt..

I felt happy when..

....

Friday

Today I felt..

I felt calm when...

....

Saturday

Today I felt……………………………………………………………………………

The best bit of today was………………………………………………………

……………………………………………………………………………………………

……………………………………………………………………………………………

Sunday

Today I felt……………………………………………………………………………

Keeping a feelings journal has been…………………………………………

……………………………………………………………………………………………

……………………………………………………………………………………………

PART 3: IT'S OK TO BE ME

GET MOVING!

Your body is amazing, and you can move it in all sorts of different ways. Enjoying your body and moving it in ways that feel good to you is a big part of accepting yourself, and it's great for letting go of perfectionist thoughts. That's because when you let your body move in any way it likes (instead of following instructions) it's impossible to get it right or wrong!

Here are some ideas to get you started:

- How do your fingers want to wriggle?
- Do your shoulders want to go up and down, or in circles?
- Would it feel good to swing your knees from side to side?
- How do your arms want to move?
- Which parts of you feel like stretching?
- Perhaps your mouth wants to sing?

I LIKE BEING ME

Can you draw yourself dancing like Coco?

PART 3: IT'S OK TO BE ME

ACTIVITY: DRAW YOUR HAPPY PLACE!

A happy place is somewhere you can imagine being any time you need a boost. Your happy place is somewhere you feel calm, happy and like you can just be yourself – there's no need to be perfect in your happy place!

Your happy place might be somewhere you've been, a space in your home, or somewhere you've imagined or seen in a book. Take some time to think about it, then draw it here:

What is the name of your happy place?

_____

_____

I LIKE BEING ME

Are there other people or animals in your happy place, or is it just for you?

_____

_____

_____

_____

_____

What kinds of things could you do in your happy place?

_____

_____

_____

_____

_____

PART 3: IT'S OK TO BE ME

GETTING COMFY WITH NOT KNOWING

Our brain always likes to try and work out what's going to happen next. This is because it's our brain's job to keep us safe. If you know what's going to happen next, you can plan for it and never make a mistake or get hurt. The trouble is, we can't know the future – not even with our very clever brains!

Perfectionist thoughts tell us we should already have things figured out, so it can feel really uncomfortable when we don't know what's going to happen.

Coco is having a birthday party at the beach this weekend! It might be sunny, but it might rain – nobody knows. If it's a sunny day, Coco's party will go ahead. If it's raining, the party can't happen.

Coco feels anxious about the weather and excited about the party – the anxious feelings mixed with excitement are very uncomfortable. Coco just wants to know for sure if the party will happen!

How could Coco deal with these uncomfortable feelings?

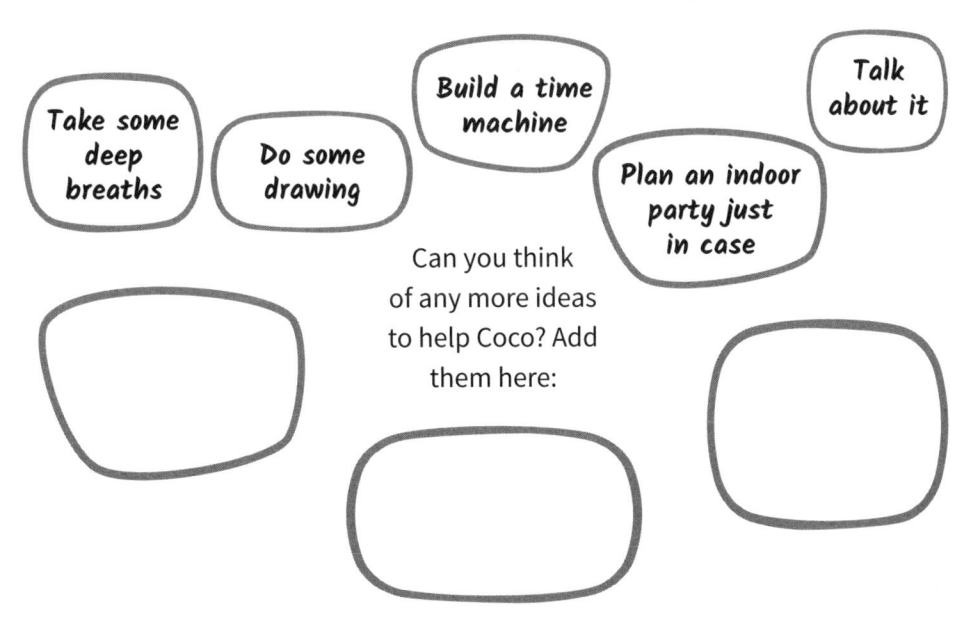

- Take some deep breaths
- Do some drawing
- Build a time machine
- Plan an indoor party just in case
- Talk about it

Can you think of any more ideas to help Coco? Add them here:

SELF-ACCEPTANCE AT SCHOOL

School can be a tricky place for feeling OK with ourselves – there are rules, grades and lots of other kids around that we might want to fit in with. Because of this, perfectionist thoughts and unhelpful behaviours can come up a lot at school.

Perfectionist thoughts and feelings about school could look like:

- 💜 I'm scared to ask for help with my work.

- 💜 I feel anxious when I'm getting ready for school.

- 💜 I feel angry when I make a mistake.

- 💜 If I don't do my work perfectly I'll be in trouble.

- 💜 I'm scared to put my hand up in case I get laughed at.

- 💜 I need to be like everybody else or I won't have friends.

That's why it's a good idea to have a few favourite calming activities you can use any time you spot those perfectionist thoughts while you're at school – think of them as a calming kit you keep in your mind.

PART 3: IT'S OK TO BE ME

Pick three activities for your school calming kit:

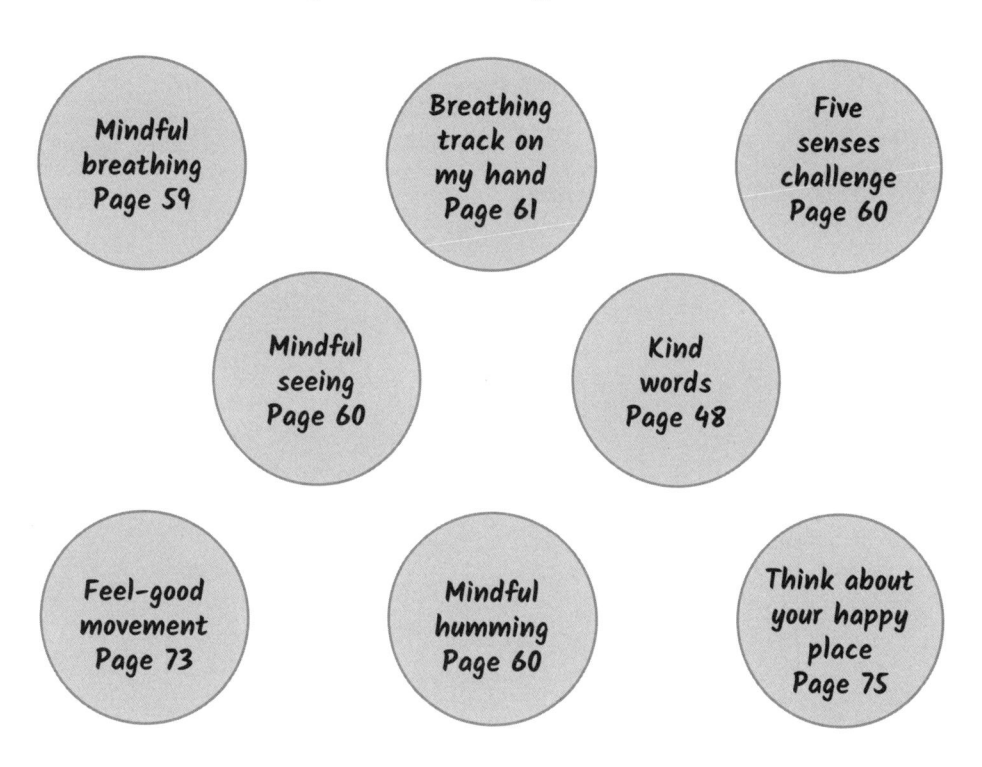

- Mindful breathing
  Page 59
- Breathing track on my hand
  Page 61
- Five senses challenge
  Page 60
- Mindful seeing
  Page 60
- Kind words
  Page 48
- Feel-good movement
  Page 73
- Mindful humming
  Page 60
- Think about your happy place
  Page 75

Write your choices here:

My School Calming Kit

1. _____
2. _____
3. _____

I CAN DO HARD THINGS

PART 4: GOODBYE PERFECT!

Now we've learned some ways to help deal with perfectionist thoughts when they pop into our minds, it's time to find out how to build up our self-acceptance so we feel good about being ourselves – even when it's hard. In this chapter you'll find ideas and activities for getting rid of perfectionism.

I am enough

I LIKE BEING ME

WHAT I CAN AND CAN'T CONTROL

Wouldn't it be amazing if you could control the weather, time or the rules at school? You could have lots of fun with a magic power like that. But it might also be quite hard work being in charge of everything. In real life, the only thing you can control is you!

That's pretty good news for self-acceptance. It can be easy to feel worried, angry or scared about things you can't control – especially if perfectionist thoughts make you think everything should be perfect! Remembering that other people are responsible for themselves (and things like time and the weather aren't within anybody's control), helps us relax and focus on just being ourselves and doing our best.

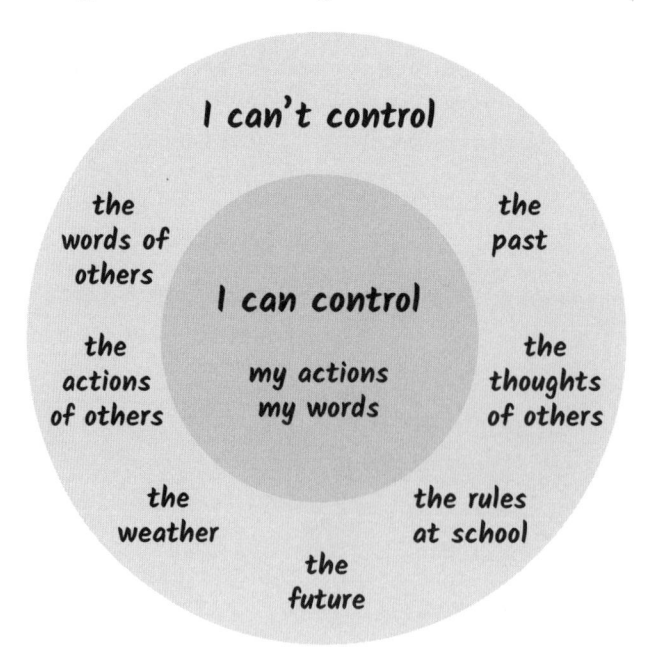

I can't control
- the words of others
- the past
- the actions of others
- the thoughts of others
- the weather
- the rules at school
- the future

I can control
- my actions
- my words

If you're worrying about something you can't control, try writing it in the outer circle here. Writing worries down helps give our brain a break from thinking about them.

PART 4: GOODBYE PERFECT!

HOW TO PRESS PAUSE

Pressing pause lets us stop and think mindfully about our thoughts and feelings. It's hard to press pause on our actions when we're feeling big emotions, but with practice, it gets easier.

You can practice pressing pause any time; here's how to do it:

♥ Imagine you have a remote control that has power over your emotions.

♥ When you feel an emotion building, you can press pause so you have a moment to think mindfully.

♥ When your emotions are paused, you can work out if the thoughts you're having are fair or perfectionist. You can take a deep breath and find some kind, self-accepting words for yourself.

♥ You can press play when you feel calm and ready.

I LIKE BEING ME

Colour in the remote control and add numbers and symbols to the buttons. If you could give your remote control other powers, what would they be?

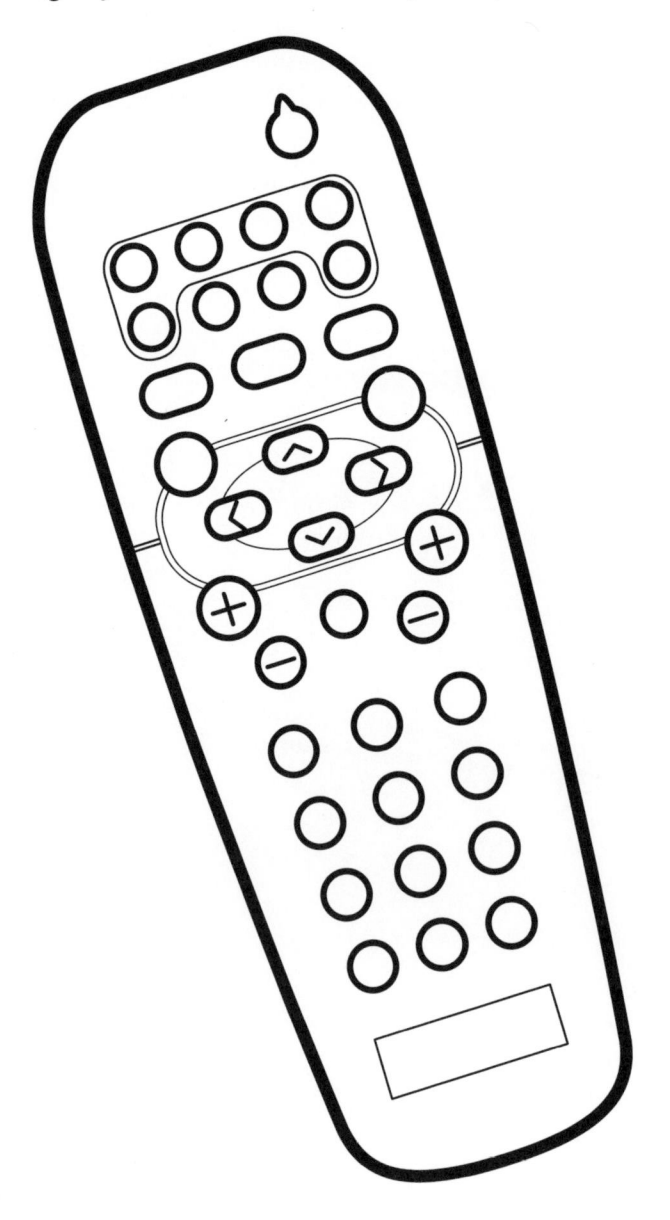

PART 4: GOODBYE PERFECT!

THINKING DIFFERENTLY ABOUT MISTAKES

Getting something wrong, or not doing something as well as you'd hoped, is part of life. Everybody – from babies to kids your age to grown-ups – makes mistakes.

Mistakes are actually really useful for learning. Imagine if you picked up a guitar for the first time ever and instantly knew how to play it perfectly. That would be so cool!

The trouble is you wouldn't understand how the strings worked, how to write your own music, what all the notes are called or how to teach someone else. That's because when we try something new and make lots of small mistakes, we learn how to do it a little bit better the next time. The times we get it perfect feel amazing, but they don't help us learn because without practice being perfect is just good luck.

I LIKE BEING ME

Learning to play guitar slowly, by making lots of really useful mistakes, is how all the most brilliant guitar players became so brilliant. The same goes for authors, bakers, artists, coders, sportspeople, teachers… in fact, anyone who is good at something became good at it through making lots of mistakes.

Making useful mistakes is how we learn!

Can you think of something you have learned slowly by practising and making useful mistakes? It could be a magic trick, drawing a character, playing an instrument… write your idea here:

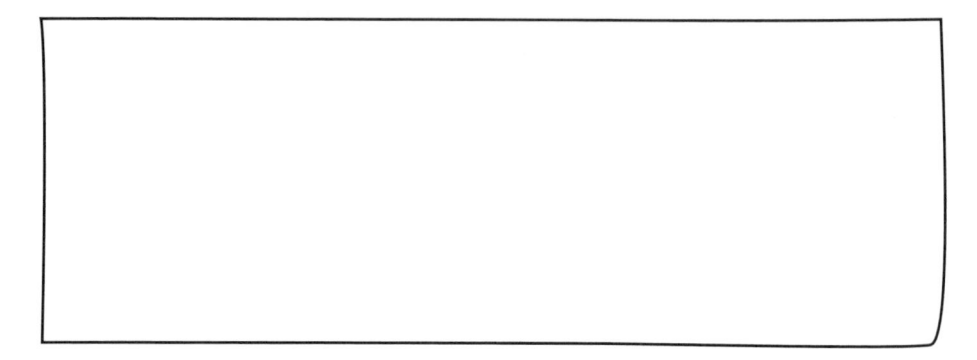

PART 4: GOODBYE PERFECT!

USEFUL MISTAKES

When you think about mistakes being useful, it feels a little bit easier when they happen. It doesn't feel good to make a mistake, but that's precisely what makes them so useful for learning – our brains remember tricky feelings more clearly than nice feelings.

So, when we make mistakes and it feels tricky, we can:

♥ Take a deep breath

♥ Remember that it's OK to feel big feelings

♥ Speak to and about ourselves kindly

♥ Get curious about how the mistake is useful

Just like everybody else, Coco makes mistakes and isn't perfect. Once, Coco got a line wrong while practising the school play.

Coco took a big, deep breath.

Coco remembered that even though things felt really hard, it was OK.

Coco said: "Think of all the lines I didn't forget! I'm doing a good job and making mistakes is how I learn."

I LIKE BEING ME

Coco got curious:

I'll remember that line even more clearly than the others now – this is what practising is for!

Can you think of a time you made a mistake? Can you find a way it was useful? Write or draw about it here.

MISTAKES ARE HOW WE LEARN!

I LIKE BEING ME

BEING YOURSELF

When we have perfectionist thoughts, it can be quite hard to be ourselves when we're with other people – even our friends! That's because perfectionist thoughts make you believe that disagreeing or not matching with other people is a big problem.

Just like mistakes, having disagreements or even arguments with our friends isn't a problem – as long as everybody is respectful and we don't hurt each other. When we disagree, it just means we've found a way in which we are different from our friend. Because everybody is unique, there are always going to be differences.

Coco's favourite lesson at school is science.

Fiz's favourite lesson is art.

Fiz is talking about all the reasons why art is the best lesson in Fizz's opinion.

PART 4: GOODBYE PERFECT!

Coco notices a perfectionist thought: *I should agree or Fiz won't be my friend any more!*

Coco takes a deep breath and lets the perfectionist thought go. It's OK to disagree! Coco and Fiz don't need to match and it's interesting to hear about Fiz's opinions.

When Fiz is finished, Coco talks about why science is the best lesson.

Fiz likes hearing Coco's opinion too.

What's the best lesson at school, in your opinion?

_____

Can you write down three reasons why you think it's the best?

1. _____

2. _____

3. _____

Perhaps your favourite is different to your friend's favourite – and that's OK. As long as we treat each other with respect, we can disagree about all sorts of things.

I LIKE BEING ME

ACTIVITY: GET CREATIVE

Being creative is a really powerful way of beating perfectionist thoughts. That's because when you create something unique, there's no right or wrong way – it's all a fun experiment.

Using all the coloured pens, pencils, crayons and chalks you have nearby, fill this space with colours and patterns.

You could try lines, squiggles, blobs or splashes – whatever feels fun and good!

I CAN CREATE SOMETHING NEW AND UNIQUE

ACTIVITY: FINDING GRATITUDE

When we're bothered by unfair perfectionist thoughts, it gets very easy to see negative things and difficult to see positive things. If you're worrying that you're not a perfect friend, you'll be thinking of the times you didn't feel so great around your friends, rather than all the fun times you have with them.

Gratitude is a really helpful tool for dealing with perfectionist thoughts. But what is it?

Gratitude means feeling thankful for things, people and experiences we get to have. When we make an effort to find the things we feel grateful for, it gets easier to see the positive things in our lives.

Coco feels grateful for a comfy chair, a delicious apple and a funny TV show.

PART 4: GOODBYE PERFECT!

What do you feel grateful for? Write your ideas in the sunbeams – see if you can find one for every beam! You can be grateful for things happening right now, memories, things you're looking forward to, people you know, things you love to do, topics you're interested in… anything that feels positive!

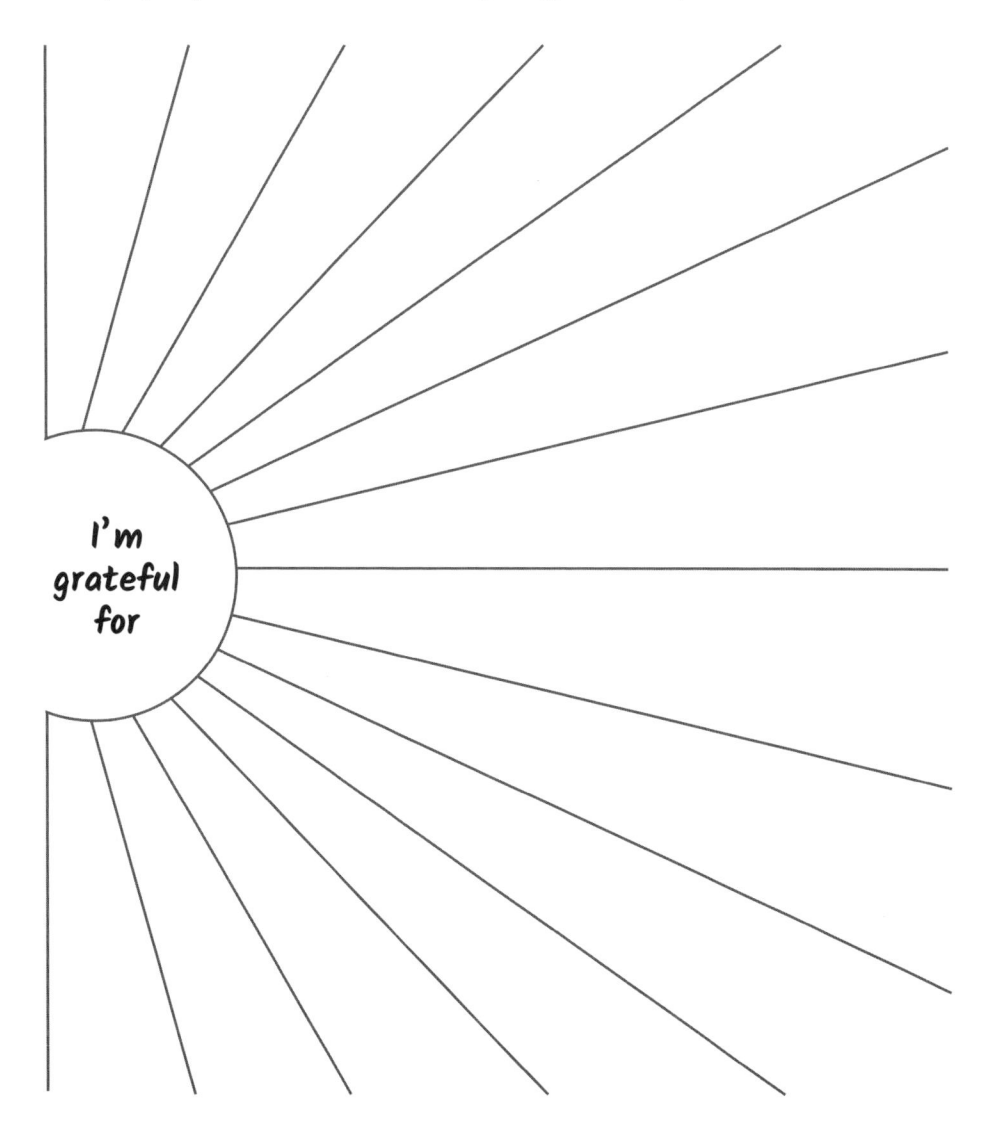

I'm grateful for

I LIKE BEING ME

ACTIVITY: WHAT IS SELF-TALK?

"Self-talk" means how we speak to and about ourselves. Our thoughts are like voices that we can hear in our minds, and how kind or unkind these voices are will make a big difference to how we feel.

Think about a time you made a mistake. Can you remember any of the thoughts you could hear in your mind? If you can, write some of them here:

For example, "I always get it wrong" or "I'll try harder next time".

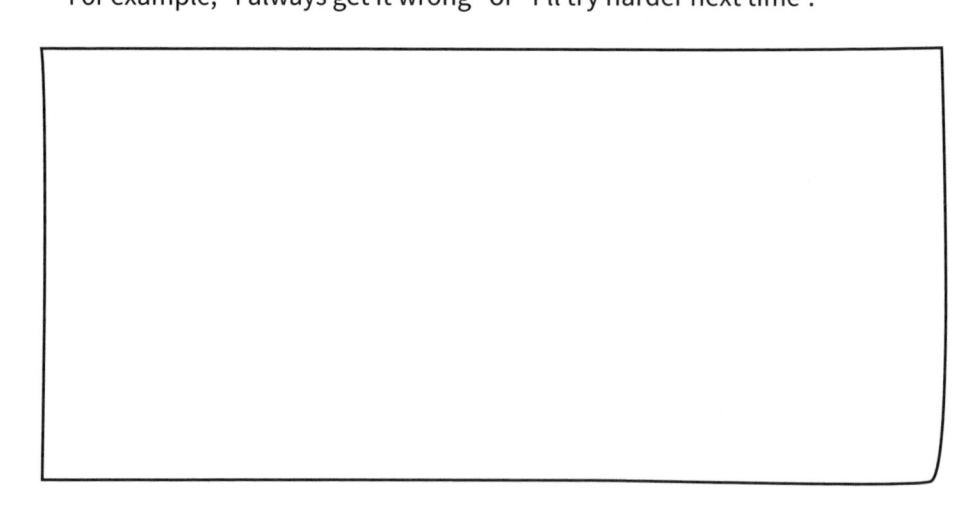

What you just wrote is an example of self-talk. How kind is your self-talk? Would you want to be friends with someone who spoke to you in that way?

PART 4: GOODBYE PERFECT!

If the answer is no, here's some good news: once you start noticing unkind self-talk, you can start to change it. Each time you spot unkind, perfectionist self-talk, you can pick a kinder thought.

For example:

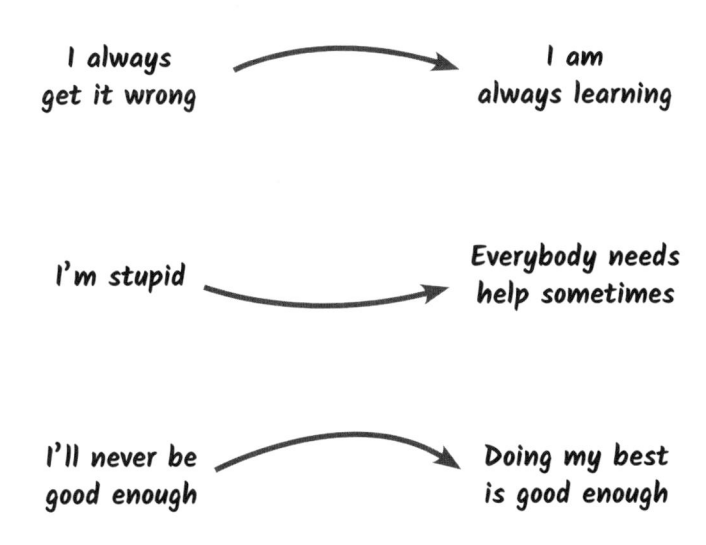

I always get it wrong → I am always learning

I'm stupid → Everybody needs help sometimes

I'll never be good enough → Doing my best is good enough

Can you think of a kinder thought to choose instead of the one you wrote on the previous page?

ACTIVITY: TELL A NEW STORY

In our heads, we're telling ourselves stories all day long! Sometimes we tell ourselves kind stories, and sometimes they're unkind and perfectionist.

Coco knocked over a drink at lunchtime one day.

In Coco's mind the story went:

"I'm so stupid, I shouldn't be allowed a drink."

Can you think of a different, kinder story?

How about:

"I feel embarrassed! I didn't mean to spill the drink, but I can help clean it up. It was an accident and it's going to be OK."

PART 4: GOODBYE PERFECT!

The next day, Coco saw some friends laughing at lunch time.

In Coco's mind the story went:

"They're laughing at me because I knocked over the drink! They won't want to be friends with me any more."

Can you think of a different, kinder story for Coco?

One of the best ways to shrink perfectionist thoughts and grow self-acceptance is to remember that every thought we have is a story. We can choose to tell ourselves kind stories or unkind ones – but just because we can choose, doesn't mean it's easy! Next time you're feeling like you're not good enough, try listening to the story your thoughts are telling you and choosing one that's kinder.

I LIKE BEING ME

ACTIVITY: GET SCRIBBLING

Coco has filled this page with a giant scribble! It was fun to get really messy and creative. Can you colour in the gaps in Coco's scribble? Try to colour outside the lines and make the scribble even more creative!

PART 4: GOODBYE PERFECT!

> You can make your own scribble picture any time, all you need is a pencil and paper. Try to be as messy as possible with your scribbling. If perfectionist thoughts are bugging you, this is a great way to deal with them!

I LIKE BEING ME

SELF-ACCEPTANCE TOOL KIT

Wow! You've learned so much about perfectionist thoughts and self-acceptance. Which activities and ideas feel most helpful for you? Put them in your self-acceptance tool kit!

When I feel like I need to be perfect, I can do…

_____

_____

I can remember that…

_____

_____

I can ask for help from…

_____

_____

I AM BRAVE

PART 5: TAKING CARE OF YOU

The kinder we are to our body and mind, the easier it gets to relax and like ourselves as we are. In this chapter you'll find out why looking after you is so important and how it helps beat perfectionist thoughts.

PART 5: TAKING CARE OF YOU

HOW ARE YOU DOING?

Learning about emotions and perfectionist thoughts is hard work and you're doing really well! It's a good idea to take a moment to think about how you are feeling every now and again. Not because there's a problem or your emotions need to change, but just to notice yourself, because your feelings matter.

How do you feel? What are you thinking about? Write or draw about it here:

I LIKE BEING ME

ACTIVITY: YOGA STRETCHES

We've already learned how brilliant moving your body is for calming big feelings – but you don't need to save it just for those tricky moments! Exercising every day will help your body grow strong and healthy, and it also helps your mind relax.

When you exercise, your brain releases feel-good chemicals that lower stress and tension. When you wiggle, run and jump around, your troubles don't seem so bad.

Yoga is a type of exercise that's about slowly stretching your body in ways that feel good to you. There's no such thing as perfect when it comes to yoga, which makes it a brilliant exercise for getting rid of perfectionist thoughts.

Try these yoga stretches:

Child's pose

Kneel on the floor with your bottom resting on your feet and lower your face to the floor. See how it feels to have your arms by your sides, then stretch them forward. Notice how they feel different. Which feels best for you?

Cat and cow

Begin on your hands and knees, then push your shoulders and bottom upward, and your tummy down. Then, push your back upward, and your shoulders and bottom down. Notice how they feel different. Which feels best for you?

PART 5: TAKING CARE OF YOU

Warrior

Bend one knee and straighten the other leg behind you. Reach your hands up to the ceiling and look forward. Now stretch your arms wide and turn to the side. Notice how they feel different. Which feels best for you?

Triangle

Stand with your feet wide, stretch one hand down to your toes and the other up to the ceiling. See how it feels to look down, forward and up. See how it feels to bend your knee, or rest your top hand on the back of your head. Notice how each movement makes the stretch feel different. Which feels best for you?

I LIKE BEING ME

MAKING TIME TO CHILL

Perfectionist thoughts can make us believe that we always have to be working hard and trying to be perfect. That doesn't leave much time for chilling out! Having time to relax every day is really important for all sorts of reasons:

- ♥ It helps you sleep better
- ♥ It makes you feel less worried
- ♥ It helps you think more clearly

Plan something relaxing every day. It could be reading, playing quietly, watching TV, walking, drawing… however you like to chill out.

How will you relax each day this week? Plan your chill-out time using this planner:

Day	Chill-out time	Chill-out activity
Monday		
Tuesday		

PART 5: TAKING CARE OF YOU

Day	Chill-out time	Chill-out activity
Wednesday		
Thursday		
Friday		
Saturday		
Sunday		

I AM
CREATIVE

PART 5: TAKING CARE OF YOU

ACTIVITY: PAINT A MESSY MONSTER

Here's a fun art activity where perfection is impossible! Have fun painting on the next page, then close the book and open it again to turn the paint into a symmetrical monster picture.

You will need:

- Paint in 1, 2 or 3 colours
- Paintbrush

How to:

1. On the next page, use your paintbrush to make a colourful splodge of paint. To make one big monster, put plenty of paint on the left-hand page.
2. While the paint is still wet, close the book and press it firmly down with your hands.
3. Next, open the book again to see your picture.
4. To make it into a monster, add eyes, arms and legs using your paint brush – or wait until the paint is dry and use pens or pencils!

Here are some monsters to give you inspiration:

I LIKE BEING ME

PART 5: TAKING CARE OF YOU

I LIKE BEING ME

YUMMY, HEALTHY FOOD

Eating a good range of food is a big part of taking care of your body and mind. When you feed your body what it needs, you feel better able to cope with big feelings.

Listen to your body – it is very wise and will tell you when it's hungry and when it's had enough to eat!

PART 5: TAKING CARE OF YOU

ACTIVITY: BUILD YOUR OWN BRUSCHETTA

This recipe is delicious and made for experiments! Bruschetta is an Italian food, with delicious things piled on to bread. Every bruschetta is unique and different, plus they're fun to make.

You will need:

- 5 slices of any type of bread

- 5 tomatoes

- A handful of fresh basil leaves, torn

- 1 clove of garlic, peeled

- Olive oil for drizzling

- Optional extras: grated cheese, salad leaves, sliced olives, cooked peas, grated carrot, diced cucumber

How to:

1. Toast your slices of bread in a toaster or in the oven for ten minutes at 180ºC/350ºF/gas mark 4.
2. While it's toasting, ask a grown-up to help you carefully chop the tomatoes and prepare any of the optional extras.
3. Ask a grown-up to help you take the toasted bread out of the oven.
4. When the toasted bread has cooled a little bit, rub the peeled garlic clove all over both sides.

I LIKE BEING ME

5. Put the toasted bread on a big plate and put tomatoes and any extras on – you can experiment with how much you add to each piece and which toppings you put together.
6. Tear and sprinkle the basil leaves over the bruschetta, and very carefully drizzle with a little bit of olive oil.
7. Now your bruschetta is ready to eat!

This recipe is for a savoury bruschetta, but you can put anything you like on top! Try a breakfast bruschetta with sliced avocado and scrambled eggs, or leave out the garlic and try a fruity bruschetta with sliced apple and torn-up mint leaves. Have fun experimenting!

PART 5: TAKING CARE OF YOU

SCREEN-FREE TIME

Using a computer, tablet, phone or watching TV is fun, and there are loads of interesting and useful things the internet, films and TV shows can help us with.

But screen time can also make it harder to fall asleep and more difficult to concentrate. What's more, the adverts and images we see on the internet can make us compare ourselves with other people. This leads us to feel more negative about ourselves and believe perfectionist thoughts. That's why it's important to balance screen time with time away from screens.

Here are some fun screen-free activities to enjoy:

- Play a board game
- Get together for a doodle session
- Care for your garden, or grow something from a seed
- Learn a card trick
- Write a comic
- Play Would You Rather? (see next page)

Would You Rather?

This is a fun game you can play with two or more people. Use your imagination to come up with your own would-you-rather questions to make the game endless.

Simply ask the people you're playing with to choose one of two options. Every question begins with the words, "Would you rather…" and you can be as silly, serious and funny as you like! There are no right or wrong answers in this game, and you can always change your mind.

Here are some would-you-rather questions to get you started:

- Would you rather live in a snail's shell or drive a car with a big worm for a steering wheel?

- Would you rather have a toe where your tongue should be or tongues where your toes should be?

- Would you rather only be able to shout or only be able to whisper?

- Would you rather be able to fly or be able to breathe underwater?

- Would you rather be a kitten or a puppy?

PART 5: TAKING CARE OF YOU

GETTING A GOOD NIGHT'S SLEEP

Sleep is very important for feeling good about yourself. When you've had enough sleep, you feel calmer and more ready for the day.

Sometimes it's tricky to fall asleep – if we feel worried, uncomfortable or just not quite tired enough, falling asleep can be tough.

Here's a trick to help you fall asleep when it's difficult:

When you're in bed, get cosy under the covers and pay attention to your earlobes. How do they feel? How about your chin? Close your eyes and slowly pay attention to each little part of your body, one after the other, from the top of your head to the soles of your feet. This will help your body and mind feel relaxed and sleepy.

I LIKE BEING ME

ASKING FOR HELP

We all need help feeling good about ourselves sometimes. It can feel scary to talk about something you're having trouble with – especially if there's an inner meanie telling you that you shouldn't need help with anything!

Any time you feel upset, confused or stuck – whether it's about a friendship, school work, a problem at home or just a feeling – you can talk about it with a friend or trusted grown-up and ask for help working it out. You are not alone!

Can I talk to you about something?

I DESERVE
TO SHINE

PART 6: CELEBRATE YOURSELF

You've made it to the final chapter of the book! You've learned so much about self-acceptance and now it's time to put it into action. In this chapter you'll find lots of ideas for using the things you've learned in your everyday life, and sharing respect and self-acceptance with others.

I am great!

PART 6: CELEBRATE YOURSELF

I'M PROUD OF...

Self-acceptance means feeling OK with being yourself, even when it's hard. One great way to feel good about yourself every day is to find something you're proud of yourself for.

It could be small or big, funny or serious. Here are some ideas:

I'm proud of myself because…

- I'm a good pet owner
- I tried my best today
- I told a funny joke
- I was kind to my friend today
- I learned a new coding technique
- I have a big imagination
- I designed a game today

I LIKE BEING ME

Now it's your turn! Fill the stars with things you are proud of:

PART 6: CELEBRATE YOURSELF

ACTIVITY: SPREAD SELF-ACCEPTANCE

Colour in this poster and carefully cut it out. Stick it up somewhere others will see it – like a window or fridge door – so you can share its positive message.

I LIKE BEING ME

PART 6: CELEBRATE YOURSELF

PLAYING YOUR PART

Nobody can take care of our community, friends and planet all by themselves! Making a positive difference in the world means everybody playing their part and working together. Here are some ideas for doing your bit to make the world a better place:

Taking part in a litter pick or beach clean	Watering trees in your neighbourhood with your grown-up
Collecting food waste for composting	Donating your unwanted clothes and toys to charity
Encouraging your friends when they feel down about themselves	Being kind and respectful to everyone you meet

I LIKE MYSELF

PART 6: CELEBRATE YOURSELF

HELPING YOUR FRIENDS

Now you know all about perfectionist thoughts and self-acceptance, you'll be able to spot when your friends aren't being fair to themselves!

If your friend speaks about themselves unkindly or seems scared of making mistakes or disagreeing, you can help them accept themselves with some kind words:

- I love learning about what makes you unique
- Hey, that's my friend you're talking about!
- Everybody makes mistakes, it's how we learn
- I found that tricky too – shall we work it out together?
- It's OK to think differently – we don't need to match
- I really like being your friend!

I LIKE BEING ME

If you have a friend who struggles with perfectionist thoughts, why not give them a Brilliant Friend award? Get a piece of paper and some coloured pens or crayons. You can copy the award certificate below, or design your own certificate. Colour in the award and write down three reasons you feel lucky to be their friend, then give it to them.

Brilliant Friend Award

I'm lucky to be your friend because:

1.

2.

3.

PART 6: CELEBRATE YOURSELF

MAKE A PROMISE TO YOURSELF

Will you do anything differently after reading this book? Perhaps you'll use kinder words to speak to yourself, or take a moment to pause when you're feeling a big emotion.

Write a promise to yourself here, about how you'll treat yourself with respect and self-acceptance:

I promise…

I LIKE BEING ME GOLDEN RULES

- Speak kindly to and about yourself
- Remember that mistakes are useful
- Be patient with yourself
- All emotions are OK
- Show respect to everyone you meet
- You are brilliant, just as you are

PART 6: CELEBRATE YOURSELF

STORIES OF SELF-ACCEPTANCE

> On the way to my friend's house, I fell off my bike and grazed my leg really badly. I felt so embarrassed I didn't tell my friend the whole time I was there, even though it hurt pretty bad – and I pushed my bike home afterward. When my carer saw the graze she cleaned it up and put a plaster on. I felt really anxious about riding my bike again, in case I fell off. My carer helped me feel confident enough to try again. I was a bit shaky at first because I was scared, but after a few minutes I was fine. It's OK to feel nervous after getting hurt and it's alright to need a bit of help.
> Luke, 11

> I always make sure that I'm early for school, because I don't like to rush. I used to think I'd get in big trouble if I was late, so I would get up extra early every morning and feel worried all the way to school. One morning, I got a nosebleed and we needed to wait for it to finish before going to school. Mum showed me how to hold the tissue and helped me keep calm. I was late for school, but it was OK and after that it didn't feel so scary. I still don't like getting nosebleeds though! Sometimes people get held up and it's not their fault. Being late is not the end of the world.
> Ava, 7

> *My friend is really good at drawing and he showed me how to draw a dog so it looks really realistic. I couldn't get mine quite as good as his and I got really frustrated with my drawing. I kept rubbing parts out and drawing them again, and it was just making the picture worse and worse as I got more and more angry. In the end I screwed up the paper and threw it in the bin. My friend showed me the video tutorial he learned from, where you can pause and rewind so it's easier to follow. I practised with the video and it felt much easier and calmer. Now I like sharing my drawings with my friend and learning from each other – it's OK not to be perfect first time.*
> Sufiya, 9

> *I got a skateboard for my birthday and thought it would be easy to learn tricks. I felt so disappointed when I only managed to roll along the pavement on my first go. I wanted to give up but my big brother took me to the skate park and I saw that all the older kids fall off and mess up the tricks they're learning too. Now I get it – messing up is part of getting good at something.*
> Hugo, 10

> *Maths is my least favourite lesson, because I find it really hard. We were learning about equations, and I just couldn't understand how it all worked – the letters and numbers just didn't make any sense to me. I thought I'd get in trouble so I didn't put my hand up and sneaked a look at my friend's work so I could see what to write. When we got some homework I just guessed the answers and afterward my teacher asked to speak to me after class. I felt sure that I was in big trouble for not understanding, but she spent time helping me understand and was really kind about it.*
> Mia, 11

PART 6: CELEBRATE YOURSELF

THE END

Coco's learned so much about self-acceptance. Have you? You can come back to this book any time you like – whether you need a boost during a tough time, to help a friend understand perfectionist thoughts or just to refresh your memory. You've worked really hard and should be extremely proud of yourself. Don't forget: when you show yourself kindness and understanding, you find your inner spark!

I DON'T NEED TO BE PERFECT, I JUST NEED TO BE ME!

For parents and carers: How to help build your child's self-acceptance

Perfectionism is something many of us struggle with in adulthood. The pressures of modern life make it feel like there's no room for mistakes or imperfection, and children feel this anxiety around not meeting the mark too. Accepting ourselves for who we are means getting comfortable with not being perfect and feeling OK about making mistakes.

The best thing you can do to help your child cultivate a healthy sense of self-acceptance is to model it yourself. When you get something wrong – big or small – use it as an opportunity to show your child how these moments can be dealt with kindly and with compassion for ourselves. Talk about a time you were resilient enough to keep trying after messing up or failing – things like driving or baking are perfect examples.

How you respond to your child is important too. When your child asks for your help with something they're learning, aim to praise the process rather than the results – draw attention to the experimentation and how they're learning from mistakes made along the way. When they mess up, act out or make mistakes, avoid shame and use these moments as an opportunity to help them put things right – whether it's a knocked-over drink or hurtful words. When children know they can redeem themselves after messing up, it's easier for them to be kind to themselves and learn the valuable lessons mistakes bring.

Help your child to accept their emotions by helping them express their feelings in healthy ways. Talk about feelings – positive and negative ones, for all family members – often in your home and allow all emotions, while staying firm around which behaviours are OK and which aren't. For example, if your child feels angry you didn't buy them a toy from the shop, you can empathize with their anger and tell them it's OK to feel angry with you, without buying them a toy or even agreeing with them that you should have. If their anger turns into hurtful words, then it's time to set a boundary around the behaviour.

Children are more resilient and learn so much more when they aren't afraid to get it wrong, ask for help and be their true selves. Self-acceptance is a lifelong skill that we're all navigating every day, and you're doing a great job by giving your child the tools to accept themselves as a brilliant, brave, imperfect young person.

I really hope you and your child have found this book useful. It's always hard when your child is struggling, and learning about emotions and how to deal with them will help them grow strong, kind and resilient. On the next few pages you'll find suggestions for further reading and advice. Wishing you all the best of luck – your child is lucky to have you on their team!

Further advice

If you're worried about your child's mental health, or you think they need extra support with regulating their emotions, do talk it through with your doctor. While almost all children will struggle with angry feelings, some may need extra help. There are lots of great resources out there for information and guidance on children's mental health:

YoungMinds Parents' Helpline (UK)
www.youngminds.org.uk
0808 802 5544

BBC Bitesize (UK)
www.bbc.co.uk/bitesize/support

Childline (UK)
www.childline.org.uk
0800 1111

Child Mind Institute (USA)
www.childmind.org

The Youth Mental Health Project (USA)
www.ymhproject.org

Recommended reading

For children:
Wreck This Journal
by Keri Smith

The Girl Who Never Made Mistakes
by Gary Rubinstein and Mark Pett

Be Amazing: An Inspiring Guide to Being Your Own Champion
by Chris Hoy

Be Yourself: Why It's Great to Be You by Poppy O'Neill

For parents:
It's OK Not to Share, and Other Renegade Rules for Raising Competent and Compassionate Kids
by Heather Shumaker

Good Inside: A Practical Guide to Becoming the Parent You Want to Be
by Becky Kennedy

Credits

pp.12, 13, 20, 25, 26, 29, 31, 41, 42, 44, 56, 58, 66, 74, 81, 83, 85, 86, 88, 90, 94, 98, 104, 111, 112, 114, 119, 120, 122, 135 – monsters © mers1na/Shutterstock.com; p.18 – outlines © Sudowoodo/Shutterstock.com; p.20 – tomato plant © Kazakova Maryia/Shutterstock.com; p.31 – ice cream © Aleks Melnik/Shutterstock.com; p.32 – inner meanie © Erik D/Shutterstock.com; pp.36, 37 – ice cream sundaes © Kate Garyuk/Shutterstock.com; p.41 – surfboard © x.designer/Shutterstock.com; p.41 – wave © Luis Line/Shutterstock.com; p.42 – rosette © veronawinner/Shutterstock.com; p.42 – painting easel © IrynMerry/Shutterstock.com; p.44 – books © bsd studio/Shutterstock.com; p.74 – music notes © WarmWorld/Shutterstock.com; p.83 – small remote control © HasebaIcon/Shutterstock.com; p.84 – large remote control © vectorisland/Shutterstock.com; pp.85, 86 – guitar © Matyushkins/Shutterstock.com; p.94 – living room © Ladusya/Shutterstock.com; p.94 – apple © RedKoala/Shutterstock.com; p.98 – spilled drink © owatta/Shutterstock.com; p.102 – toolbox © Fresh_Studio/Shutterstock.com; pp.106, 107 – yoga poses © Maquiladora/Shutterstock.com; p.114 – healthy food © mhatzapa/Shutterstock.com; p.116 – bruschetta © aidan_aly/Shutterstock.com; p.119 – bedroom © Ksenya Savva/Shutterstock.com; p.135 – sparklers © GzP_Design/Shutterstock.com

Other books in the series...

Be Brave — A Child's Guide to Overcoming Shyness
Poppy O'Neill
Paperback
ISBN: 978-1-78783-699-0

Be Strong — You Are Braver Than You Think
Poppy O'Neill
Paperback
ISBN: 978-1-78783-607-5

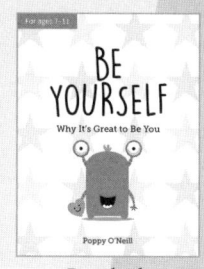

Be Yourself — Why It's Great to Be You
Poppy O'Neill
Paperback
ISBN: 978-1-78783-608-2

Be Cool, Be You — A Child's Guide to Making Friends
Poppy O'Neill
Paperback
ISBN: 978-1-80007-339-5

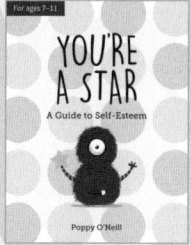

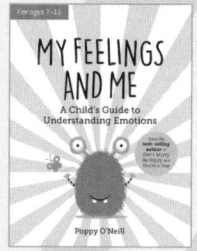

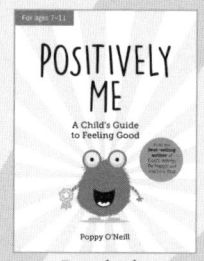

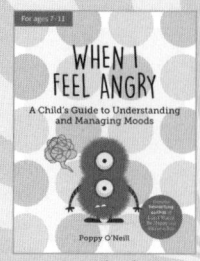

Don't Worry, Be Happy — A Child's Guide to Overcoming Anxiety
Poppy O'Neill
Paperback
ISBN: 978-1-78685-236-6

You're a Star — A Guide to Self-Esteem
Poppy O'Neill
Paperback
ISBN: 978-1-78685-235-9

My Feelings and Me — A Child's Guide to Understanding Emotions
Poppy O'Neill
Paperback
ISBN: 978-1-80007-338-8

Positively Me — A Child's Guide to Feeling Good
Poppy O'Neill
Paperback
ISBN: 978-1-80007-169-8

Be Mindful — A Child's Guide to Being Present
Poppy O'Neill
Paperback
ISBN: 978-1-80007-710-2

When I Feel Angry — A Child's Guide to Understanding and Managing Moods
Poppy O'Neill
Paperback
ISBN: 978-1-80007-690-7

Be Calm — A Child's Guide to Feeling Relaxed and Happy
Poppy O'Neill
Paperback
ISBN: 978-1-80007-711-9

You Can Do Amazing Things — A Child's Guide to Dealing with Change and New Challenges
Poppy O'Neill
Paperback
ISBN: 978-1-80007-340-1

Other Vie books for parents, carers and children...

Paperback
ISBN: 978-1-80007-421-7

Paperback
ISBN: 978-1-80007-423-1

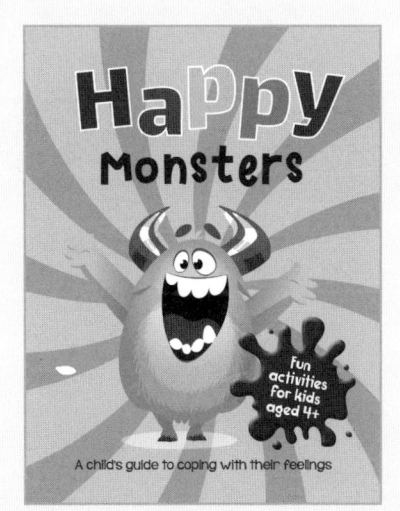

Paperback
ISBN: 978-1-80007-422-4

Paperback
ISBN: 978-1-80007-559-7

Have you enjoyed this book?
If so, why not write a review on your favourite website?

If you're interested in finding out more about our books, find us on Facebook at **Summersdale Publishers,** on Twitter at **@Summersdale** and on Instagram at **@summersdalebooks** and get in touch.
We'd love to hear from you!

Thanks very much for buying this Summersdale book.

www.summersdale.com